Managing
Credit and Credit Cards

NO NONSENSE FINANCIAL GUIDE™

Managing
Credit and
Credit Cards

Andrew Ambraziejus

Cover design by Nancy Sabato
Interior design by Richard Oriolo

ISBN: 0-681-41496-0

Printed in United States of America

First Edition

0 9 8 7 6 5 4 3 2 1

Acknowledgments

The author would like to thank the following people for volunteering their time and information: Kerry Ashton, Chester Dalzell, Jim Donahue, Jon Gartner, Patrick Hubert, Rene Kellybreen, Norman G. Magnuson, Sylvia Smithson.

Contents

Acquiring and Managing Credit: A Rite of Passage

Acquiring and managing credit is one of the most important rites of passage in our society. It is also one of the most neglected. Parents, overwhelmed by the ever-changing rules and regulations of dealing with creditors, and by their own struggles with paying the bills, don't seem capable of adequately teaching the concept of credit to their children. Colleges offer many courses on economic theory yet precious few on personal finance management. Unprepared, a young man or woman enters the working world and is bombarded with credit card applications and the promise of easy money. The temptation to start living on credit—as though that in itself is a sign of adulthood—is great. But as one young woman deeply in debt remarked, "What comes after is anybody's guess."

While the borrowing boom of the 1980s has abated, turning into the recession-plagued 1990s, the lure of buying on credit is very much alive. Trying to recover from their own losses from bad loans, banks and other financial institutions are striving harder than ever to come up with new ways of making money in the one area that has continued to do well for them: issuing credit cards. For those who find themselves in financial trouble, preapproved cash advances, cheap loans, special bank accounts, and other methods of getting quick cash are advertised daily on radio and TV. And the junk mail never stops, promising easy credit to all.

While all these advertisements trumpet the ease with which one can get credit, the *cost* of the credit is hidden in the fine print. A 2 percent monthly minimum payment of the outstanding balance on a cash advance sounds reasonable, but when you read carefully, you realize the annual interest rate works out to 22 percent. No annual fee for the first year with a low interest rate sounds like a great deal for a credit card—until a year later, when the annual fee is charged and the interest rate turns out to be fluctuating up, not down.

Scared off by stories of financial ruin and bankruptcy, many are tempted to do away with credit altogether: never take out a loan, cut up the plastic, pay for everything in cash. The problem with this way of thinking, of course, is that living without credit in our modern society means living on its fringes, not being able to borrow money for basic necessities. Whether you like it or not, you must face the fact that credit is here to stay.

The answer lies in neither extreme: you do not want to be a slave to credit, nor a stranger to it. You want to learn how to use credit intelligently, to make it work for you. The scare stories and problems aside, there are real benefits to using credit and credit cards. In this book you will find out what these benefits are and how to make good use of them.

PART I

Credit and the Credit Process

1

Keeping a Good Credit Rating and Establishing Your Financial Future

Other People's Money was a hit play of the money-happy 1980s. Detailing the buyout of an unprofitable, family-owned New England manufacturing company by a hard-hitting Wall Street "raider," the play pointed out the very real conflicts between making money and holding on to certain societal values. Its theme can be applied to every consumer on a personal level: the first thing to remember when you get credit of any kind is that credit is *other people's money*. Credit may provide gratification now—it may get you out of a financial hole or allow you to take a vacation or invest in something that you hope will reap great rewards in the future—but whatever the outcome as you strive for that goal, you are using someone else's money.

Forgetting this is the first and biggest mistake many of us make when someone extends credit to us. Overlooking it is easy because your reasons for needing the money may seem legitimate or pressing at the time: the credit is needed for a medical emergency, for education, or to buy something you have wanted for a long time which is now on sale. No matter how noble the purpose, however, the money will have to be repaid.

Remember, banks and other financial institutions make money on credit—a lot of money. When a bank gives you a loan, it also charges you interest. That is why the bank is giving you a loan in the first place—it knows it will make money off you. It doesn't care what your purpose is for borrowing the money; it only cares that you pay it back.

Think of credit as an agreement: the bank agrees to lend you some of its money, and you promise to repay this money in keeping with the terms and interest rates to which you agreed. If the system works well, both parties benefit: you get money that you otherwise would not have, and the bank makes a profit.

Why do you need credit? Because of the way our society is structured, you will need to borrow money at various times of your life. How many of us can afford to put down cash for a house or a car, or send a child to college without borrowing money? Even major appliances and pieces of furniture are often bought on credit. In addition, day-to-day living is getting harder and harder without the purchasing power credit cards provide: making reservations, getting tickets, shopping by phone, and paying various bills are made that much easier by using plastic. Yes, it is possible to live without credit and credit cards, but in order to take full advantage of the benefits living in this society provides, credit is indispensable.

What Is a Credit Rating?

There is another very important component to credit. Without it, getting credit would be impossible. That component is your credit rating.

Currently there are about 900 credit bureaus in this country that keep track of our debt repayment habits. The information that the bureaus sell to creditors is the credit (or consumer) report. The majority of the credit bureaus use one of the information systems maintained by three companies. Known as the Big Three of the credit reporting industry, these companies maintain among them files on an estimated 170 million Americans and generate 1.5 million credit reports *per day*. The three companies are:

- TRW, Inc., in Orange, California
- Trans Union Corporation in Chicago, Illinois
- Equifax in Atlanta, Georgia

The Big Three compete with each other to get the business of the banks, financial institutions, and retailers who grant credit. Because they deal with so many credit-granting businesses, chances are very good that one of the Big Three companies has credit information on you.

Any institution that is thinking of lending you money immediately looks at the credit report generated by one of the three companies to determine whether you will get a loan. Your credit report is a financial report card of sorts that every lender looks at carefully. If there is negative information on the report, your chances of getting a loan are diminished accordingly.

Having no credit rating is as unfortunate as having a bad one. Banks want to know that you are a responsible consumer—that you know how to borrow money and pay it back. Seeing a record of good payments provides the bank with the assurance to give you new, bigger loans. That's why financial counselors talk about the important concept of building a credit history. You won't get a significant loan without any history to back yourself up. But if you keep your credit rating in good standing over the long run, you will have no problem borrowing money for those important items that you will need later in life.

Your Credit Report—What's in It?

In general, your credit report will be made up of the following types of information:

1. Personal identifying data
2. Account information
3. Matters of public record
4. An inquiry section

The first item includes information for identification purposes: your address, social security number, employer, etc. Given the millions of reports generated by the credit bureaus, mistakes have occurred in mixing up reports and the people who receive them. The mistakes often seem small and unimportant, but with millions of records, small mistakes become big headaches. With improvements in computer software, the credit bureaus promise that such problems will be greatly reduced.

The main body of information in a credit report pertains to your different accounts. It describes the accounts you have and tells your credit grantors how you pay your bills. The information includes such specifics as the following:

- The name of each company that has granted you credit
- The nature, or type, of account you have with each company (a revolving credit account; an account you have to pay off each month; an installment account of fixed payments every month)
- Who is legally responsible for the account, such as a joint versus an individual account
- The particulars of every account: when it was opened, your balance, credit limit, amounts past due
- Your payment profile—typically, numbers are assigned to each month of payment; for example, *1* reflects a payment that was made on time, *2* means you were 30 days late, *3* means you were 60 days late, and so on
- Dates of last activity on an account
- How long the account has been reported
- A statement giving the status of the account (the account is with a collection agency; an account is

in dispute; an account is inactive; a credit card has been reported stolen)
- Additional information, such as former addresses and employers

Usually there is also a section that contains matters of public record, that is, court information. Such information includes tax liens, bankruptcy declarations, lawsuits, judgments against you. Local, state, or federal courts are identified, along with any court codes or docket numbers.

The inquiry section lists businesses that have received your credit report in the last two years and may include such information as the kind of credit or loan you applied for, its terms, and amount. This section tells the potential loan grantor how many other businesses you may have approached for loans in the recent past.

Whoever is thinking of extending you credit will have a pretty comprehensive picture of not only your financial status, but legal and personal matters as well. Using this credit report, and the information you provide on any application for a loan or credit card, a business thinking of extending credit to you will make decisions as to how much money to lend and under what terms. The credit reporting agencies themselves do not make recommendations about extending credit. Their job is to provide the information that others use.

Establishing Credit

"Whether you like it or not, living as a full, functioning member of this society means learning to master different levels of credit."

These are the words of a budget counselor who wishes there was a personal finance course taught in every high school in the country. "It's so helpful for young people to learn about budgeting in simple, un-threatening ways," he adds. "Not as something 'out there' or 'for others,' but for them. If they learn to view it as a series of steps, one leading to the next, like climbing a staircase, they begin to appreciate the impact that credit has on their lives."

The metaphor of a staircase is a good one. Establishing credit takes time, patience, and responsibility—and it's something for all of us, not just the select few who are "good with this sort of thing." Realizing that establishing credit is a long process, made up of many small steps rather than a sudden leap into financial decision making, helps take away some of the fear of learning to integrate credit into our lives. Whether we're teaching our kids or trying to put our own financial house in order, it's a metaphor to keep in mind.

And what are those first steps? If you're a young person just starting out, or somebody trying to build credit from scratch after bankruptcy or other misfortune, it can often feel as though you need to have credit to get credit. While this is certainly true at certain levels of borrowing, there are things you can do to start establishing a good name with creditors when you have little or no previous credit history.

Open up checking and savings accounts at your local bank and get into the habit of paying certain things by check. Your purchases probably won't be for large amounts, and they shouldn't be. At this point, your main concern is to establish yourself as a valued, responsible customer with the bank.

Also, once you open an account, try to establish a good rapport with at least one person who works in the customer service area. Go over and ask questions from time to time about any services the bank provides, its rates of interest, or anything else you would like to find out about. You may not think it important in the beginning when you are just dealing with various tellers and making ordinary deposits and withdrawals. But if in the future you should have a problem, or want a loan, or have another special need, having somebody that knows you will only help matters.

Trying to get a small personal loan, of perhaps $500 or $1,000, that you know you can pay back is another route to take. Open up a savings account with the money you borrow and then use it to pay the loan back over time. This will cost you some money in interest, but you will show your bank that you are a good credit risk. A report of your timely payments will appear on your credit report as well.

In using a loan to improve your credit rating, be careful to use the money for repayments instead of buying something with it. Human nature being what it is, when you get a sizable amount of money in one lump sum, it is very easy to discover many things that you suddenly just can't live without. Resist the temptation, or else your plan for creating a good credit standing for yourself will backfire.

Besides bank loans, other avenues are open to you in establishing a good credit record. In addition to the emotional rewards, getting one's first home or apartment is also an important step toward financial responsibility. When you put your name on a lease or become a paying customer of the phone or electric company, you're giving yourself a chance to establish credit. If your first home away from home is a shared situation with a number of roommates, try to have your name on record with at least one utility company.

Another fairly easy route to establishing a credit history is getting a department store charge card. Eager for new customers, department stores give them out without too much fuss. They know that once people have charge cards, they will come to the store and shop with them. (They will spend more money, too. Various studies show that people using charge cards spend more than those paying by other means.)

The ease with which you can run up charges is, of course, one of the dangers of the department store card: you can purchase anything at any time without a penny in your wallet. It is tempting to abuse this privilege, whether cheering yourself up after a bad day at the office or just window-shopping and impulsively buying an item that grabs your fancy.

If you run into problems with the convenience a department store card provides, a way to avoid this trap is to bring your card with you only when you are going to the store to look for a specific item. Don't have your card with you when you're going "just to look around" or "check out the sales." This will cut down on impulse buying, yet you will still have your card when you truly need it.

Another danger of a department store card is high interest charges; they're often higher than your average

Visa or MasterCard. However, like the other cards, department store cards also have grace periods, so that if you pay your bill right away you can avoid finance charges.

With a charge account at a department store, you become a preferred customer, receiving notices of upcoming sales and various other promotions before the general public. If you see something advertised that you've been wanting to buy, you will be in a better position to find exactly what you're looking for. If you are dissatisfied with an item, you can return it before you've paid your bill, which is a real advantage of any credit card.

All in all, a department store card is a good investment. To establish some credit, buy a few small items and pay your bill when it comes in. Do it several times over the course of the year to keep your account current. If your account is good, your credit limit will be increased and so will your purchasing power.

Finally, consider getting a gasoline card. Gasoline cards are not very difficult to acquire and the danger of running up charges is not too great, since you would use a gas card in more limited circumstances.

Discrimination and Credit

Throughout this book, reference will be made to a number of laws that have been passed in recent years to make sure the consumer gets fair treatment regarding credit. Understanding your rights under these laws will help you protect yourself and know what actions you are entitled to take in various situations. Become acquainted with the basic tenets of each law. It may save you problems in future situations.

In 1975, the Equal Credit Opportunity Act became law in this country. While the law allows any creditor to examine the facets of your life that will directly influence your credit-worthiness, it does not allow the creditor to make certain assumptions based on characteristics such as: sex, marital status, religion, ethnic status or national origin, race, age, or whether you get public or private assistance.

In other words, just because you are unmarried, or just because you are sixty-five years of age, you cannot be automatically denied any kind of loan. Of course, other factors may convince a creditor you are not a good credit risk, and they may be legitimate. The point of the law is that everyone gets the same treatment.

Women in particular have been helped by passage of this law. In the past, many women had trouble getting credit. If they had been married and were suddenly widowed or divorced, for example, they would be shut out of the credit system because the only credit history they had was a shared one with their husbands. It was too difficult for single women to get credit, because single women were not considered good credit risks. A woman applying for credit should know that under the Equal Credit Opportunity Act a creditor may not do the following:

- Inquire about birth control or plans for children; that is, a creditor may not assume that you plan to have children if you're at a particular age, or that your income will change if you do

- Refuse to consider alimony or child support if they are made on a regular basis (you only have to reveal such payments if you think it will improve your chances of getting credit)
- Refuse to consider your income if you are married, even it is just from part-time employment
- Refuse to grant an individual account if you are married
- Require a cosigner or husband's signature if you are married

Questions related to these topics are allowed, however, when they have a direct bearing on your ability to repay the loan. To get a more complete explanation of the law, write to the Office of Consumer Affairs of the Federal Deposit Insurance Corporation, which will send you various pamphlets explaining the law in greater detail (the address is listed in the appendix at the end of the book).

2

Why Borrow?
On Getting a Loan

Before you start thinking about the opportunities and consequences of various kinds of credit, take some time to sort out your feelings about borrowing money. The "rules" about when to borrow and when to hold off apply equally well to all kinds of credit. When you have sorted it all through, you will be in a better position to make intelligent choices and borrow money without getting in trouble down the line. Your calculations should take into account two basic questions:

1. What is your reason for borrowing money? The more specific your answer, the better. If it's just a vague "I need more money" or "I want to enjoy things that I've denied myself previously," you are headed for trouble. Instead of thinking about loans, you should first take a good hard look at your standard of living and work situation to see if there is any way you can cut down on expenses or increase your income.

In general, years of experience have shown lenders that the following are *good* reasons to consider a loan:

- Buying a house or car
- Buying any major appliance or piece of furniture that you will use right away, on an ongoing basis
- Borrowing for education
- Coping with a medical emergency
- Creating debt that will pay for itself (for example, borrowing for a down payment on a three-family house and using the rents to cover all payments)

On the other hand, the following are *not good* reasons for borrowing money:

- Buying something on a whim
- Paying back other debts
- Investing in get-rich-quick ventures
- Borrowing money to buy things to make yourself feel better
- Borrowing money with the expectation that you will be making more money in the future

2. What will be the consequences of borrowing money? You may have a good reason to borrow money, but if you can't make your payments, you will just create bigger problems for yourself. In determining whether to borrow, use this rule of thumb: on a monthly basis, no more than 15–20 percent of your take-home pay (after taxes) should be used to stay current on all debt payments. This rule of thumb does not include mortgage payments (use no more than 35–40 percent of *gross* monthly pay if mortgage is included) but does include payments for all charge cards and loans.

Also, remember that repayment methods on loans differ. With a regular bank loan, you work out repayment terms with the loan officer before you get a penny of the money. With an open line of credit, such as a charge card, you borrow what you need when you need it, up to your credit limit, and the repayment schedule is left up to you. Although at first having such flexibility may seem desirable, it is also a trap. It is all too easy to overlook the interest and other fees that are charged on your unpaid balances until you are in deep financial trouble.

Think through carefully how much you can realistically afford. Taking into account the 20 percent rule, compare how much money will be coming in to what your monthly payments will be. Can you live on what is left over? If your answer is yes, you can take the next step and apply for the loan.

Applying for a Loan

Once you have decided you have a legitimate need for borrowing money, you will have to apply for a loan. Whether you apply for the loan from a bank, a savings and loan association, or a credit union, the process is basically the same. You will meet with a loan officer and be asked to fill out an application. This application will have questions about your living situation, work history, education, income, assets and liabilities, as well as questions about other outstanding loans. You will also be asked why you want the loan. What the loan officer sees on your application, along with your credit report, will be the two main factors that influence the bank's decision on whether to let you borrow money.

What kind of information on a loan application sways the bank's decision in your favor? The following factors will enhance your chances:

- Living at your present address for at least a year, preferably two or three
- Working at your current job for several years
- Working at a big or established firm in your town or city
- Having an account at the bank where you are applying for the loan
- Being known for work you have done in your community
- Completing your education, the higher your degree the better

The following factors will reduce your chances of getting a loan:

- Renting a residence (as opposed to owning a home)
- Much moving around or job changing
- Having black marks on your credit rating—late payments, disputes, unfulfilled obligations, law-

suits, bankruptcy; the more serious the problem the smaller your chances

- Working on an intermittent or free-lance basis

What the positive and negative factors above translate into are *reliability* and *stability*. The loan grantor is entering into a business deal with you. He or she wants the deal to be as risk-free as possible and wants to make sure that you will be able to repay the loan on a timely basis. While there is no such thing as a perfect or correct loan application, fill it in with the loan officer's point of view in mind: the more you can show that you are responsible and able to repay money that has been loaned to you, the better your chances of getting the loan.

Also, keep in mind that a bank loan is not a handout—you should not feel intimidated asking for a loan, as if the bank is doing you a favor. It's really the other way around: by borrowing the money and making interest payments, you are providing the bank with its lifeblood, profit. So don't be afraid to ask for clarification on something you don't understand. Make sure all fees related to a loan are clearly spelled out. Remember, it never hurts to ask: if you don't like what you hear, you can take your business elsewhere.

Types of Loans

Loans are granted to suit the different needs of those who get them. Accordingly, terms, payment schedules, and interest rates can be tailored to fit the specific requirements that you may have for borrowing the money at any given time. As you search for the best deal, keep in mind that all terms are negotiable: if you already have a savings account at a particular bank, for example, find out if you can get a percentage point or two knocked off your interest rate. Often the answer will be yes.

The types of loans you can apply for are:

• **A personal loan.** This kind of loan ranges from a few hundred to thousands of dollars. You can use a personal loan for any purpose. Once you and the loan officer have agreed to the conditions of the loan, you will pay it back by making monthly payments, or installments. Generally, the interest rates will be high. The easiest way to find out the rates is by calling various banks; they will tell you whether they grant personal loans and what the rates are.

A personal loan can also be "secured"—you pledge certain assets, such as a savings account, as collateral against the loan. If you don't make your loan payments, the bank is legally allowed to take possession of those assets. Because a secured loan represents lower risk for the bank, the interest rates tend to be lower.

• **An auto loan.** Auto loans are granted by banks as well as automobile manufacturers. The manufacturer's interest rates tend to be higher; you are really paying for the convenience of the auto manufacturer acting as middle man—getting money from the bank and doing all the paperwork. Once quoted a fee by the manufacturer, compare it to what your bank can offer—if the difference is big enough, the inconvenience of getting the loan on your own may be worth it.

Remember that the shorter the term of the loan (two

or three years as opposed to four or five), the lower your interest rates. It certainly makes sense for the auto manufacturer: the sooner you pay off your car, the sooner you will start thinking of buying another one. Of course, the shorter-term loan will also carry higher monthly payments.

• **Mortgages.** A mortgage is usually the biggest loan you will ever carry. The complexities of getting a mortgage require a book of their own. The main thing to decide is whether you want a fixed-rate mortgage or an adjustable-rate mortgage, which will be a few percentage points lower to start with but can fluctuate over time. Various factors enter into this decision, such as current interest levels and how long you intend to live in the home.

In addition, you may be charged "points" on your mortgage. When discussing points, think of them as extra interest. One point equals one percent of your mortgage.

• **Home equity loans.** These loans have become very popular in the last few years. A home equity loan is really a refinancing of your current mortgage. With a home equity loan, you can borrow up to 75–80 percent of the value (or equity) of your home, minus whatever the unpaid mortgage is. The advantage of a home equity loan is that the interest rate is much lower than on a personal loan. Also, the interest is still fully tax deductible, which is no longer the case for other consumer loans, such as credit cards.

The big—very big—disadvantage of a home equity loan is that you are putting up your home as collateral. If you have any trouble making your loan payments, you could lose what is the biggest investment you have. With this in mind, most experts caution you to tread carefully. Consider a home equity loan only for major expenses that cannot be avoided, such as emergency medical care or financing a child's college education.

• **Student loan.** Higher education is a major expense, one that the average student—or parent—cannot afford without taking out a loan. Tailored specifically for those seeking a way to pay for their education, student loans have low interest rates and don't have to be paid back until you leave school or graduate.

All institutions of higher learning offer their own loan or financial aid packages that you have to apply for separately if you want to be considered for aid. The federal government also provides help in the form of loans, grants, and work study programs to qualified students. All these financial aid programs and how you can apply for them are listed in a booklet called "Financial Aid from the U.S. Department of Education." To receive a free copy, call the toll-free number (1-800-433-3243).

Credit Unions

Frequently overlooked, credit unions are a good source of loans, often providing them at lower rates than banks.

Credit unions differ from banks in a number of important ways. They are nonprofit organizations and are governed by a different set of laws and regulations. A credit union is owned by a group of individuals who have banded together out of a common interest. This common interest could be the workplace, a church, labor union, professional or civic organization, or a community cooperative. A credit union is democratically run and managed by its members, who all have a vote. The first credit unions in this country were formed in New England in the early years of this century. Right now, there are nearly 15,000 of them in the United States, with more than 69 million members.

Although no two credit unions function exactly alike, in general they provide services similar to those of banks. You can open savings accounts (or "shares"—at a credit union shares represent your ownership); checking (share draft) accounts; and, depending on the size and assets of the credit union, the following may be provided: IRAs, credit cards, loans, certificates of deposit, direct deposit of paychecks, traveler's checks, and a host of other services. Although credit union interest rates on loans tend to be lower, your assets are insured up to $100,000, the same as at commercial and savings banks.

Most credit unions are members of state leagues, which in turn all belong to the Credit Union National Association (CUNA). To find out about credit unions in your area, look in the yellow pages under credit unions. Or, you can write to the national association (address is listed in the appendix), which will be happy to send pamphlets and give you the address of the credit union league in your home state.

PART II

Credit Cards

3

The Credit Cards You Can Get and How They Work

In acquiring any credit card, you should always take an active role. The credit card market is exploding at present, and many companies will issue you credit cards, each seemingly more attractive than the next. All the companies have different sales pitches and offer different interest rates, billing procedures, and bonuses or perks. You will have many decisions to make.

This chapter will help you make them and will explain that, lucky for you, it is a buyer's market. You are in control and don't have to take every card that comes your way. There are many cards to choose from and, as an intelligent user of credit, you will want to examine each carefully and acquire the cards that are right for you.

A Short History of Credit Cards

In January 1952, a short article ran in *The New York Times* that began with the following sentence: "Anyone who can sign his name and pay his bills can charge his way through some of the better hotels, restaurants, and night-clubs of the country under a new credit card system known as Diners Club." Founded two years earlier, Diners Club had an annual fee of $5, and members got a small booklet that listed the establishments where the card was honored. Other credit cards, such as those issued by department stores, gasoline and airline companies, had been issued for years, but Diners Club responded to the growing need for a card that would be accepted by more than one establishment within a particular industry.

Diners Club quickly established itself in the early fifties. In 1958, American Express, the financial services company, issued its own travel and entertainment card. Meanwhile, banks were experimenting with their own cards. The Bank of America in California issued its BankAmerica card, later to become Visa, and in the sixties, what is now MasterCard was founded. The credit card explosion had begun.

During the 1970s and 1980s, credit card use sky-rocketed. Visa and MasterCard became the dominant bank cards, and American Express became the recog-

nized leader of what is now called the travel and entertainment card. In the mid-eighties, there came a realization that we were borrowing too much. Congress
passed the Tax Reform Act in 1986. One of its provisions
was that interest on credit card payments would be
slowly phased out as a tax deduction (it ended completely
in 1991). Then came the stock market crash of October
1987, the Wall Street scandals, the Savings and Loan
scandal, and the recession of the early 1990s. Loans came
due that couldn't be paid and bankruptcies went up,
making everyone self-conscious about their borrowing
habits.

Sensing a new consumer awareness of the price
consumers have been paying for shopping on credit,
many companies, such as AT&T and Sears Roebuck,
decided to issue their own credit cards, trying to lure
customers with lower fees and greater discounts. The
banks, having suffered many losses, are fighting back,
coming up with their own discounts and perks. Even
prestige-conscious American Express has admitted to
problems and is starting a campaign to win back its
upscale business clientele.

What does all this mean for the consumer? While
there will be many changes as new cards and marketing
ideas come and go, there will also be opportunities. If you
know what to watch for and keep in mind that you have a
choice—a *wide* choice—you can make the credit card
system work for you.

What to Look For—Read the Fine Print

Even though you will see many marketing pitches and offers in an attempt to sell you on one credit card over another, the basics don't vary. Pay careful attention to them, and tailor the rest to your particular needs. The basics are:

1. The Annual Percentage Rate (APR). This is the interest you will be charged on any unpaid balances if you have a card that provides revolving credit. Keep in mind that the interest rate can either be fixed or fluctuate over time, as banks may add a certain percentage to the prevailing prime interest rate or other economic indicators to come up with their APR. If you get a card with a low interest rate that fluctuates, keep periodic tabs on it.

2. Annual Fee. Most creditors now charge annual fees in the $15–$30 range ($55 for American Express) for regular cards and $50–$75 for gold cards.

3. The float, or grace period. A major attraction of credit cards, the grace period allows 25–30 days of no interest charges before your payments are due.

4. Special transaction or late fees. Typical fees include those on cash advances and late payment fees.

While it shouldn't be at the top of your shopping list, the fact that banks have many different ways of figuring your monthly interest is something you should know. The average daily balance method is popular and acceptable, and does as the name implies: it averages your daily balance and applies the interest to it. This method may include or exclude purchases you made during the month; if it excludes purchases you are not being charged interest on them, which is a good deal for you. Other methods calculate the interest on beginning or ending balances. If you pay off your account in full every month, of course, the interest won't matter anyway.

The Fair Credit and Charge Card Disclosure Act, passed in 1988, stipulates that all credit card issuers list the above information in a uniform, legible manner. However, various loopholes exist. For example, the rules apply to anyone soliciting you; that is, all the mail you receive advertising various cards, preapproved or not, should list that information. But if you try to get a card on your own initiative, by going down to the local bank, for example, these rules don't strictly apply. Don't be surprised if bank personnel try stalling you or tempting you to apply first and ask questions later. Resist such tactics. In this day and age, when the competition for credit card business is fierce, you are more than likely to find a helpful bank. A way around the problem is to look for brochures advertising credit cards, which should have the information printed in a table format, another requirement of the Fair Credit and Charge Card Disclosure Act.

Always pay attention to the fine print, because that is where the real differences between the cards are spelled out. Unfortunately, it is still legal to make the fine print so small you may need a magnifying glass to read it. Make the effort. Being aware of the basics should cut down on the time involved and allow you to go beyond the hype to find out the real costs of each card.

Types of Cards—What's Available

We have already discussed gasoline and department store credit cards as a good way of establishing credit. While they are relatively easy to get, they have one big limitation when compared to more generally recognized cards such as Visa or American Express: they can only be used at the particular vendor that issues them. If you happen to be in another store or gasoline station, you have to use another method of payment.

This convenience is at the heart of the marketing of the generally recognized cards; each claim worldwide acceptance. For the average consumer, there are now three types of these cards to choose from:

- Bank cards, such as Visa and MasterCard
- Bank-type cards (issued by nonbanks)
- Travel and entertainment cards, such as American Express and Diners Club

Bank cards. As the name implies, bank cards are issued by banks. Their outstanding feature is revolving credit—you don't have to pay off your balances in full each month. However, for that privilege you pay interest.

The most important thing to remember when shopping for a Visa or MasterCard is that cards with the same name are not necessarily the same. MasterCard and Visa are essentially networks or associations of various banks that have banded together to facilitate credit card processing. Because banks are controlled by different state laws, the cards they issue all have different interest rates and fee structures. Therefore, what matters is the particular bank that is issuing the card.

How do these cards work? The customer makes a purchase for, say, fifty dollars with the credit card. A processing bank buys the signed credit slip from the retailer for, in this case, $48.90. This $1.10 loss to the retailer represents the fee the retailer is charged to belong to the Visa or MasterCard network (2.2 percent in this example). The processing bank, in turn, sells the slip—working through the Visa or MasterCard network—to the bank that originally issued the card for a price of $49.30. By selling the credit slip at a slightly higher price ($49.30) than it paid for it ($48.90), the processing bank makes a profit. The issuing bank makes a profit, too, because the customer will be charged the full $50 for the purchase, plus any interest charges.

The end result of all this? The retailers get your business, both banks make a profit, and you've taken home merchandise that you haven't yet paid for.

In addition to making a profit from the discounts at which they acquire the credit slips, banks make money in other ways. Most important, because bank cards have revolving credit, the banks make money on the interest they charge you on unpaid balances. They also make money from annual membership fees, as well as various transaction and other charges.

The advantages to you of a bank card?

• **They are widely accepted.** Their convenience factor is great. Aside from your local merchant, other industries that you may not have considered, such as hospitals, supermarkets, taxicab companies, even movie theaters, are accepting bank cards to varying degrees.

• **You get a float or grace period after you purchase an item before payment is due.** Usually, this float period is 25 to 30 days. If you buy an item at the beginning of a billing period, you extend the float to nearly 60 days. This allows you to use your money for other purposes or keep it in the bank for interest.

You should know, however, that once you have an unpaid balance on a credit card, you can be charged interest immediately on all new purchases, without the benefit of the grace period that you had when you made your first transactions.

• **You don't have to pay off your full balance every month.** This is the great advantage and *dis*advantage of the bank card. If you really need something immediately and don't have the cash, a credit card is wonderful. The disadvantage is that you can get into this frame of mind constantly and charge thousands of dollars before you ever think of making substantial repayments.

Related to this danger are the very high interest rates you pay. When banks pay you an average of 5 percent interest on your savings and you are paying them 15 to 22 percent, the arithmetic shows who is getting the better deal. As noted in chapter 1, bank cards are also issued by credit unions, often at lower rates. If you are able to join a credit union, you may get a very good deal.

Because of the intense competition for your business, all credit card issuers are coming up with more perks to grab your attention. One of the most popular currently offered is variously known by such names as Price Assurance or Price Protection. These programs allow you to get money back if you see a product you have bought with your card advertised for a lower price. These programs have various restrictions such as the advertisement having to appear in print within a certain number of days of your purchase; check with the card issuer on the particulars so you know what to look for.

Credit card issuers have also started offering insurance on your minimum monthly payments. If some disaster strikes and you can't make minimum payments for a while, you can purchase insurance that freezes your account; you don't have to make your monthly payments and you won't ruin your all-important credit rating. Various limitations and hefty fees for this privilege vary from state to state, so before signing on for such insurance, think it through carefully. If you are already in financial trouble, you don't need to pile more debt onto your account.

Examples of some other perks:

- Extended warranties on items you purchase
- Discounts on long distance phone calls
- Additional car and travel insurance.

Bank-type cards. Another interesting development for the consumer in the last few years has been the issuance of bank-type cards (that is, cards with revolving credit) by other companies. The front-runners right now are the Discover card issued by the retailer Sears, Roebuck and Co., and the Universal card, which is a Visa or MasterCard issued by the communications giant AT&T.

As with cards issued by banks, both of these cards are not limited to one type of establishment or industry, and both offer the standard 25-day grace period to repay a balance. Interest rates are often in the high range. There is one major difference from your standard Visa or

MasterCard. As a marketing tool to attract customers, both cards have been offered without an annual fee—for life. How long this feature will be offered probably depends on how many customers each card acquires, but if you are thinking about getting one, be sure to ask. Everything else being equal, why pay an annual fee if you don't have to?

As an added bonus, AT&T's Universal card offers discounts on long distance calls and can be used as a calling card. The Sears Discover card offers cash rebates of up to one percent depending on how much you charge each year. Its main drawback is that it is not yet as widely accepted as your standard Visa or MasterCard.

To further confuse matters—and give you yet another choice—American Express has launched its own revolving-credit card, the Optima Card. It, too, has a standard grace period, an annual fee (if you have a regular American Express card the fee is lower—$15 as opposed to $25), and charges interest on any unpaid balance. The Optima card's advantage: Since American Express is trying to win customers for the card, its interest rate tends to be lower than that of the other cards.

With the market in such flux, all these cards are certainly worth considering, perhaps as an adjunct to your primary card(s). When the market sorts itself out, you can make a better decision as to which cards you want to keep.

Travel and entertainment cards. The most well known of these cards are American Express, Diners Club, and Carte Blanche (which started as a Hilton Hotels card in 1959).

The significant difference between bank cards and

travel and entertainment cards is that you do not get revolving credit; that is, you have to pay back your balance in full each month. As their name suggests, travel and entertainment cards have also historically been narrower in scope than bank cards. Since its inception in 1958, the American Express card had always been identified as a card for use in nice restaurants and for travel and business purposes. Although that has changed in recent years, as all credit cards have broadened their services, the scope of travel and entertainment cards is still not quite as wide as that of bank cards.

Travel and entertainment cards also don't preset spending limits the way bank cards do. However, you should know that your monthly spending habits are monitored. If you normally charge $200 a month on your American Express card and suddenly start charging thousands, you can be sure headquarters will want to know what is going on.

Another strong lure of these cards is prestige. Through a successful marketing campaign, owning an American Express card, for example, has come to be viewed by many people as a real rite of passage: to be able to whip out that green card with friends or business acquaintances means that you have arrived both professionally and financially. The fact that one has to pay a comparatively high annual fee for this prestige does not seem to bother anyone.

Should you try to acquire one of these cards? Again, you have to think about your needs and spending habits. If you tend to be undisciplined with your payments, being required to pay back your balance each month can be viewed as a definite advantage—no worry about interest rates. If you conduct a lot of business entertaining and spend a fair amount of time traveling, a travel and entertainment card provides you with many conveniences. American Express offers a Membership Miles program, for example, in which members can earn one frequent flyer mile for every dollar charged with the American Express card. (Check with American Express, 1-800-297-1095 to find out which airlines currently participate in the program.) Also, your monthly statement includes a photocopy of your credit slip, which is a help for more accurate record keeping. If you're a world traveler, your travel and entertainment cards will be accepted at fine establishments and will expedite getting emergency cash, services, and information.

The downside is the high annual fee, which is double or triple the average bank card. (If you use the card extensively for work, check with your personnel office; some companies will reimburse your annual fee.)

Cash Advances

Another service that credit card issuers provide is the ability to get a cash advance. You simply walk into a bank, produce your card, sign a slip, and walk out with a sum of money that is charged against your credit card. It's as easy as that. It's also very dangerous.

Since the procedure for obtaining a cash advance is very similar to buying something at a store, most people assume the charges are the same. However, cash advances are generally much more expensive:

• **The interest can be higher than on regular purchases.**

• **You get no grace period with cash advances; interest is charged immediately.**

• **Many banks charge a transaction fee for every cash advance.** Typically, this fee is 2–3 percent of the amount you have been advanced. (Remember, this is on top of the regular interest you will be paying for borrowing the money.)

These factors make cash advances a very expensive proposition indeed. And these extra charges will not be readily advertised.

The obvious advantage of a cash advance is that old Achilles' heel, convenience. If you are away from home and need money, it will be there for you (provided you haven't charged your card to its limit). Cash advances can also help in emergencies.

So tread carefully. Only borrow on a cash advance if you know that you will be able to pay back the money within a very short time.

Gold Cards

Successful . . . rewards . . . lifestyle . . . select group . . . exclusive . . . deserve . . . service . . . unique privileges . . . specially selected . . . status . . .

These buzzwords taken from gold card advertisements tell you what these cards are all about. Are they worthwhile? Not for the average consumer. Why pay money for something (in the form of a higher annual fee of 50 to 75 dollars) when you are not going to need most of the unique privileges being offered?

Although the interest rate on gold cards tends to be lower than on their more plebeian cousins, this isn't a good enough reason to get a gold card. If you're already expecting to run up high monthly balances, no matter how much lower the interest—and it's usually a few percentage points lower, say 17.4 instead of 19.7—think again: unless you know you can repay those balances within a short period of time, you're headed for trouble.

Prestige? To some people it may seem worthwhile. What might be more worthwhile are the higher credit limits and various perks offered on gold cards. With intense marketing wars between companies, new perks such as no annual fee, higher credit limits, and no charges for various services are advertised every day. If you are considering a gold card, as always, read the fine print! For example, one brochure extolling the virtues of a particular card blithely invites members in good standing to skip some payments. A tiny asterisk beside the word *payments* leads one to the tiny type on the last page where one is reminded that the interest charges continue to accrue—as always. Back to reality.

Here are some other examples of the perks that are being offered with gold cards. Before you jump to apply, note that many of these perks are now finding their way to regular cards—yet another good reason to shop around.

- A year-end summary of all transactions, to help with record keeping and income tax.
- Copies of your receipts with your monthly statement

- Car rental insurance that supplements existing policies (you can also decline the collision damage waiver offered by the car rental company, which can save you money)
- Higher limits on travel insurance
- Higher warranties
- Various services such as getting a second card free or the opportunity to purchase hard-to-get tickets to various cultural and sporting events

Are these perks worth the annual fee? You will have to decide.

Finding Cards with the Lowest Interest Rates

For a list of cards with low interest rates, contact Bankcard Holders of America (BHA). Located in Herndon, Virginia, BHA is a nonprofit consumer organization founded in 1980 to help consumers deal with various credit card issues. The list costs $4.

You can also become a member of BHA. Dues are $24 per year. For that $24, you will receive the list free, plus:

- A bimonthly newsletter discussing the latest developments in the credit card area
- Pamphlets and publications on various topics educating the consumer on rights and credit card protection
- A toll-free consumer dispute hotline
- Access to a speakers bureau, offering speakers who present seminars and lectures to civic, com-

munity, and volunteer organizations at no charge

The address and telephone number for the Bank-card Holders of America can be found in the appendix.

Money and *Barron's* magazines also provide listings of low-interest cards. As you apply for the cards, however, remember that their lower interest rates are usually offset by higher annual fees.

Debit Cards

With the advance of automatic teller machines at banks and other electronic processing networks, there has appeared another new wrinkle in the plastic card industry—debit cards.

Debit cards (or money cards, as some banks are calling them) are not credit cards. What sets these cards apart from credit cards is the fact that they are tied to an account you have set up at the bank. Think of such cards as checks. You go to a store and purchase an item; the sales clerk punches in a price; you insert your card into a decoding device and punch in your personal identification number (PIN); the clerk punches another button to send all the information to a processing center, which will verify that funds are available in your account; then, the funds are taken out of your account and the sale is complete. All this takes only a few seconds.

This speed represents the main drawback of debit cards for many people. With a regular check your funds stay in your account a day or two before the check makes its way to your bank. This allows you to earn some extra interest and also stop payment if you have to. With a credit card, you have a much longer period—up to the full 25–30-day float—to keep your money earning interest to stop payment.

For those people who tend to abuse their credit cards, debit cards provide a real advantage: because the card is tied to your account, you cannot spend what you do not have. Unlike a credit card, a debit card does not allow you to charge up thousands of dollars if you don't have the money in the first place. For those who have felt the emotional burden of paying back huge credit card debts or have flirted with bankruptcy, this represents a very real plus. (If you do start relying on a debit card because of your abuse of credit cards, you will have to be careful that your card is not also tied to overdraft privileges, just as any check can be. Overdraft privileges cost you interest, and before you know it you can be in a lot of trouble again.)

Do not confuse the debit card with the automatic teller machine (ATM) card that is used to withdraw money from the cash machine. While similar, it is not the same card. The goal of banks in trying to establish debit cards is to have them used at various retail outlets that people go to on a daily basis: supermarkets, gasoline stations, movie theaters, local stores, and the like. If the cards become well established—and they appear to be taking off—they will further alleviate the need to carry around cash, which represents another convenience to many people. Not only is your billfold a little thinner, but you have greater security as well.

The Visa and MasterCard networks have also gotten into the act. By the mid 1990s, they will both introduce debit cards that will be part of the Visa or MasterCard network, which will allow them to be used nationally. Visa's debit card is called Interlink; MasterCard's is the Maestro card.

But the disadvantages of a debit card can be great, too. You will lose the grace period of a regular credit card, since your money will be taken out of your account immediately. And, just as with a regular credit card, the temptation to spend more than you really want to will be high; even if you can't spend more money that you have in your account at the moment, that may be a hollow victory. If the account is all the money you have in the world, it will still be possible to create big problems for yourself during that shopping binge or vacation spree.

So, again, think through your needs. When the advertisements for debit cards start coming, their advantages will be trumpeted. They are real, but so is the loss of float time and the temptation to overspend.

Secured Bank Cards

A secured bank card combines the features of debit and credit cards. Like a debit card, the secured credit card requires you to have an account at the bank. This account "secures" your credit card, and your credit limit is as high as the amount of money in your account. Unlike a debit card, the secured credit card operates like a regular credit card: there is a grace period of 25–30 days; you don't have to pay off your entire balance; there are annual fees and interest charges on unpaid balances.

For those who are trying to establish credit or who

have bad credit ratings, secured cards offer the possibility of getting one's foot in the door of the credit card system. One pays high interest rates and secondary charges for this privilege, and some banks add on an initial processing fee to cover the costs of checking your credit rating.

If there is no way you can get another card, consider a secured card, but by all means shop around. Compare the four basics (APR, annual fee, grace period, late and transaction fees) and ask if there is a processing fee as well. If there is a processing fee involved, make sure that it will be refunded to you if your application for the card is turned down.

For a list of secured cards, contact the Bankcard Holders of America. The cost of the list is $5. If you become a member, the list is free.

4

Your Credit Card Rights and Privileges

Knowing which credit cards to shop for is only half the battle—the other half is knowing how to use the cards to derive the full benefit from them. As dangerous as credit cards can be, they also provide advantages that shopping with cash or paying by check do not.

The two federal laws that protect your rights regarding the use of your credit cards are the Truth in Lending Act, passed in 1968, and an amendment to it, the Fair Credit Billing Act, passed in 1974. Information on these laws can be provided by the Federal Deposit Insurance

Corporation (FDIC), the federal government's banking regulatory agency. You will find the address and phone number in the appendix.

The Monthly Statement

Your monthly statement is your record keeper. Along with the copies of the credit slips you receive every time you make a credit card purchase, your monthly statement provides a way to double-check the particulars of your account. It is also a good way to check up on yourself and your use of the card during the past month.

As you go over your statement, remember that, like anything else, it is subject to human error. Wrong transactions may be listed, amounts owed or paid may be incorrect—just because it comes from a world-class bank or finance company doesn't necessarily mean everything will be perfect. As you will discover in this chapter, the recognition of this margin for error is the reason specific laws exist to help you sort out problems and correct mistakes.

Always take good care of your credit slips. Make a point of taking them out of your wallet or purse and filing them away in a safe, accessible place. When your statement comes in, take the time to match the transactions listed on it against the credit slips you have accumulated. If there is a discrepancy you have something to show the bank as proof of a problem.

Keep your monthly statements for at least a year, preferably two. They are a handy reference at tax time. At the end of each year (or beginning of the next) your card issuer should provide a figure listing your total interest payments for the year. Even though interest payments on credit cards are no longer deductible, it will be instructive for you to see just how much your charging habits have cost you over the year. Also, the list of transactions on your monthly statements will provide a handy, concise reminder of the year's tax deductible expenses.

The law also provides that specific information appear on your monthly statement. Besides the basics (name, address, account number), the most important things listed are:

- The payment due date—the date by which payment must be received to avoid late fees and the amount you must pay to avoid any further finance charges
- The minimum payment—the least amount you may pay to avoid being delinquent on your account
- The dates of the billing cycle
- Your balance both at the beginning and end of the billing period (the balance is the total amount of money you owe your card issuer)
- Your credit limit—subtracting your new balance from your credit limit tells you how much charging power (in dollars) you have left
- Each transaction, listed with the date, amount, and a brief description identifying the store and the goods or services purchased
- Any payments you made during the month— these amounts should be credited to your account

- The amount of any finance charge calculated on the account during the period—this is the interest you will be paying, plus any fees the issuer charges you
- The annual percentage rate (APR) at which your interest is calculated
- A statement describing the method of calculation for the interest rate, the balance on which the calculation was made, and whether this calculation includes new purchases or payments made during that month

An address as well as a telephone number should be listed for any questions you may have regarding your account. In addition, there should be a notice that if you call instead of write, you may forfeit some of your legal rights in regard to credit cards. The importance of these rights are discussed below.

Billing Errors

You receive your monthly statement in the mail and find a charge you do not think belongs there. After going through your credit slips, you are sure that you have discovered a billing error. What do you do to rectify the situation?

If there is a disputed amount on your statement, you don't have to pay for it until the matter is resolved. By law the credit card company can't charge you interest on the disputed amount, nor can it report you to a credit bureau as being delinquent for not making a payment.

The law also spells out a certain procedure for both you and the credit card company to follow in such a circumstance.

First, you must inform the credit card company that there has been a billing error. Important: you have to do this in writing. If you merely make a telephone call, the company isn't legally forced to do anything.

You can do both: make a telephone call, which in most cases should be enough to solve the problem, but be sure to send a follow-up note immediately. The note will protect you if a problem does develop in the future. Note these requirements in regard to sending your note:

- Send it within sixty days of receiving your statement
- State your name and account number (so that the creditor can adequately identify you)
- Indicate your belief "that the statement contains a billing error and the amount of such billing error"
- "Set forth the reasons" why you believe there is a billing error; give the particulars—you never do business with the creditor; they overcharged you by half; they added in other charges that weren't quoted beforehand

As a wrap-up, ask that the matter be taken care of promptly; and to show your credit card issuer that you know your rights and mean business, politely but firmly state that you understand you don't have to pay the disputed amount, nor should you be charged interest on it.

In order to make sure that the letter has been received, send it by certified mail, otherwise (as has happened) the credit card company can claim it never received your complaint.

After receiving your letter, the credit card company then has thirty days to either take care of the problem or send you a "written acknowledgment" that it is looking into it.

If the company decides to look into the matter, things have to be settled within ninety days of the receipt of your original notice. If the company finds you are right, it has to correct your account, credit any finance charges that might have been erroneously billed to your account, and notify you in writing that it has done so. If the company doesn't agree with you, it must send you a written explanation and, if you request, provide "copies of documentary evidence" of the charge in question.

Unfortunately, after this point the law gets hazy. If you still believe that you are right and the company's documentary evidence is somehow wrong, you can keep your campaign going by writing letters and refusing to pay. If the credit card company tries to intimidate you by threatening to report you to its credit bureau, know that you have rights in this area as well. As you will find out in the next chapter, you will have every right to give the bureau your own version of events.

Stopping Payment

Another important right you have using credit cards is being able to stop payment on merchandise you aren't happy with or services you find unsatisfactory. Evolving from the legal concept that both sides should abide by the terms of any contract between them, this right recognizes your contract with the seller: if the goods or services you paid for are not what they seemed, you have a right to get your money back. Because of the grace period paying by credit card gives you, this right is especially effective.

There is one basic stipulation to your right of stopping payment: the law requires that you make a "good faith attempt to resolve the dispute" with the actual seller before you resort to not paying your credit card bill. What does "good faith" mean? The law was left open on this; good faith efforts have to be judged according to each individual case. If you buy a camera, for example, and after finding that it doesn't work as it was advertised attempt to return the camera to the dealer and get a refund, you have acted reasonably in trying to fix the problem. Or if someone performs repairs on an appliance and it still doesn't work, and you call up asking the repairman to do more work, which he refuses, you have acted in good faith. You have a right to stop payment.

That is why paying by credit card is a good idea in many cases—it gives you that much extra time to evaluate what you have purchased before actually paying for it. You remain in control and don't have to be stuck with something that was falsely advertised, shoddily produced, or unsatisfactory in some other way.

As far as dealing with your credit card company is concerned, follow the procedures outlined above to resolve a billing error to cover yourself as fully as possible. Do everything in writing, explaining why you are stopping payment and how you tried to get the matter taken care of in good faith.

There are two other requirements stipulated by law that you should be aware of regarding stopping payment. The first stipulates that you can only stop payment for a purchase that amounts to more than $50; the second, a geographical one, stipulates that to stop payment "the place where the initial transaction occurred was in the *same state* as the mailing address previously provided by the cardholder or was *within 100 miles* from such address." The geographical requirements can get complex (where does the transaction take place if you purchase something over the telephone from an out-of-state company?), and in cases that have gone to court, the requirements have been interpreted in various ways. If your purchase falls outside the limitations, it can't hurt to try to stop payment anyway. If you're forced to pay, you haven't lost anything by trying.

Stolen Cards

When your card is stolen, or some other unauthorized use of it occurs, the *most* you are liable for under the law is $50.

The way you notify the credit card company is not spelled out in detail. According to the law, "A card issuer has been notified when such steps as may be reasonably required in the ordinary course of business to provide the card issuer with the pertinent information have been taken." In other words, you can write, make a telephone call, or do it in person at the bank. Obviously making a telephone call is the fastest and easiest method, but rest assured that timing is not crucial. That is one of your biggest protections with a credit card. Even if you discover some time after the fact that your card has been stolen (or someone has gotten hold of your number illegally), and charges are already being made on it, your total liability under the law is still only $50.

Remember, though, that a stolen card is not the only way someone can get into your account. It's really the number itself that matters, and if somebody finds your number on discarded receipts or carbon copies, that person can use the number to make purchases. To minimize this risk, always take care with receipts and carbons. Rip up carbons yourself or have them ripped up in front of you and thrown away. File credit slip receipts in a safe place, and be careful how you throw away old ones—left exposed in the garbage, for example, they can provide great temptations for others to get at your credit.

The $50 limit on liability is good news for anyone worried about stolen cards. The not-so-good news is that, as much of life, things aren't always so clear-cut. To illustrate, here is an example:

> Frustrated by work and other problems in his home city of New York, Paul decides to take a break and visit some friends in Philadelphia for the weekend. Strapped for cash at the moment and charged up to the limit on his own card, he asks his good friend Alex if he can buy his train tickets on Alex's Master-Card. Alex agrees and gives him his credit card number. Promising to pay Alex back as soon as he returns, Paul purchases his tickets and goes off to

have some fun. But he has so much fun that he spends all his money quickly and soon finds himself using Alex's MasterCard number for a lot of other purchases, running up charges of close to a thousand dollars. Although he promises to repay Alex immediately upon returning to New York, he has further financial setbacks and cannot pay. Is he legally responsible for the thousand dollar charges or is Paul?—after all, they are in Paul's name.

This is where a concept known as authorized/unauthorized use comes into play. According to the law, unauthorized use "means a use of a credit card by a person other than the cardholder who does not have actual, implied, or apparent authority for such use." In general, then, if a cardholder has authorized someone to use his card, he is responsible for any charges that have been made on it before the cardholder has notified the bank that something is wrong. (Once you notify the bank, you are clear; unfortunately, most of such charges happen beforehand.) That is why you should never give your card or its number out—you can find yourself legally responsible.

However, and this is an important *however*, a related issue is one where some of the use is authorized (in the case above, the train tickets) and some isn't (the rest of the charges). Who is legally responsible when a person previously authorized to use a card continues to use it in an unauthorized manner? (A related scenario to the one above occurs all too often during a breakup of a marriage or a relationship; one person takes the other's card and begins making charges on it.)

In the above example, a successful argument can and has been made that you are only liable for the train-ticket amount. So, if you do feel compelled to give out your card or its number to someone you know, have a very clear understanding of what and how much will be charged. But if you want any guarantees in this matter, your safest option is to keep the card exclusively for your own needs.

Debit Card Liabilities

If you have a debit or "money" card, it is important to know that the amount you may be liable for differs greatly from your liability with a credit card. The liability based on the number of days you have to notify the bank after you've learned that there has been unauthorized use of your card. With a debit card, you are responsible for the amounts as follows:

Up to $50	within 2 days of unauthorized use
Up to $500	within 60 days
Unlimited	more than 60 days

As you can see, unlike a credit card, with a debit card prompt notification of any problems is crucial. If someone gets into your account, they can take out all your money, plus use any overdraft privileges connected to it.

The personal identification number (PIN) that you are issued with any debit card is meant to protect you against a lost or stolen card. To make best (and safest) use of your PIN, keep in mind the following:

- Don't give it to anybody.
- Never keep the PIN with your card or in your wallet.
- In choosing a PIN, don't take anything obvious or that may be on your records, such as your birthday or your first name (remember, letters as well as numbers are allowed). Devise gimmicks or mnemonics that only you could know: names of relatives, numbers and names having to do with work, hobbies, a particular sequence of numbers. Be careful of making the PIN too obscure or you may have troubling remembering it yourself and may be tempted to write it down and carry it around with you.
- Always be alert to any possible scams or attempts by someone to get you to reveal your number. If you are at an automatic teller machine at a bank, for example, someone hovering around or who suddenly develops a problem with another automatic teller machine and asks to use your card to check it out may just be after something more.

Telephone Fraud

With the proliferation of electronic technology in many industries and services, new ways of committing credit card fraud have opened themselves up to unscrupulous marketers. One of the most common involves the telephone.

There is no question that charging something over the telephone to your credit card is the height of convenience. You specify the item you want, give your credit card number, and the item is yours. Tickets for cultural and sporting events, hotel reservations, or car rentals, and shopping for various goods and services can all be completed within minutes.

By and large, most of the businesses you deal with are legitimate and will pose no problems. Even so, when you do shop over the telephone, make a point to double-check the exact amount you will be charged and, just as important, the name under which the transaction will appear on your monthly statement. If you buy something from Company X, for example, and it is owned by Company Y, it just might be Company Y's name that appears on your statement. Knowing the name and the amount will help you when you go over your statement every month.

Certain firms, such as credit reporting agencies, make money by selling the information they have on consumers to other companies. The way it works: a business contacts the credit reporting agency and gives it statistics of the kind of person it is looking for to pitch a particular item (for instance, men, aged thirty to forty, making $50,000 a year, who have three credit cards). The credit bureau provides the company with a list of people who fit the profile, though they do not provide credit information per se. Using this list, the new company in turn tries to solicit business from the people whose names it has acquired.

If an unscrupulous company acquires this list, the techniques it can use to get someone's business are legally very questionable. A common ploy is to call and offer the consumer a free trial offer for an item or for a particular service. Once the consumer has agreed to the trial offer, he suddenly finds himself with a charge on his monthly credit card bill —although he has not yet agreed to purchase the item or service. If a free trial offer comes your way, make sure it is with the understanding that nothing will be charged to your account. Once you have been charged, the seller has a psychological advantage. You can stop payment, but the extra effort required to do so is what an unscrupulous seller counts on, hoping you will shrug and accept the item.

Because so much is changing so rapidly, laws about selling credit card information and other such marketing practices are not yet on the books. Various laws have been introduced in certain states, but it will be a while before their final form and any kind of national consensus will be forged. For now, your best advice is to be wary.

If you want some additional guidance when it comes to using your credit cards over the telephone, you can write for a free pamphlet called "Tips for Telephone Shopping." Put out by the Direct Marketing Association in New York City, the pamphlet tells consumers what options they have when companies contact them by phone, gives information on 900 numbers, and discusses consumer rights and safeguards. You will find the address of the Direct Marketing Association in the appendix.

Mail Solicitations

Founded in 1917, the Direct Marketing Association is a not-for-profit trade association sponsored by various businesses and nonprofit companies that advertise and sell their wares through direct market channels—by phone or mail. In addition to the pamphlet on telephone shopping mentioned above, the association offers the consumer many other services. One of them involves curtailing unsolicited or "junk" mail.

You may have wondered how you get those credit card offers in the mail, as well as other unsolicited mail advertising everything from household items to magazine subscriptions to sweepstakes offers. It is that practice of selling mailing lists, a very profitable business. If you want to cut down on mail solicitations write to the Mail Preference Service (MPS) at the Direct Marketing Association. According to its news release, the association's Mail Preference Service is free and was begun by the association in 1971 to give consumers the option to have their names removed from national mailing lists and databases. Local advertising is not affected. However, since about 80 percent of all direct mailers belong to this association, if you do choose to do this, your unsolicited mail will drop considerably. (For reasons of confidentiality and accuracy, you must write, not call. As with other Direct Marketing Association services, you will find the address for the Mail Preference Service in the appendix.)

Before you choose this option, the association advises that you consider it carefully. Studies indicate that when consumers take a minute to think about unsolicited mail, most of them like receiving it, at least to a degree. They discover that it's not junk but a way of staying in the information loop and finding out about what is available from mail order companies, credit card and financial services, publishers, and nonprofit organizations. With this in mind, the association also gives you a second, less drastic option: you can lessen unwanted mail solicitations simply by asking those companies you do keep wanting to hear from not to give your name out to other mailers. If you are currently struggling with credit card overload and don't want to tempt yourself with more offers, for example, this may be a good option for you to take.

Upon written request, the Direct Marketing Association will send you more information on these options as well as a listing of its other services, which include:

- Information on further protections offered by the Fair Credit Billing Act
- A free guide to understanding mailing lists, called "How Did They Get My Name?"
- The *Great Catalog Guide,* a resource to more than 260 direct mail catalogs in 50 product categories, $3
- The Mail Order Action Line (MOAL), started in 1981 to help consumers with mail order transactions; to get help you must write to the Mail Order Action Line at the Direct Marketing Association
- A Telephone Preference Service; similar to the Mail Preference Service, this cuts down on unwanted sales calls
- Communication by telephone for the hearing impaired; for information call (212) 297–1DMA [1362]

5

Managing
Your Credit Cards:
Know Your Limits

It is estimated that Americans currently own between 800 million and one billion credit cards. The average person has eight and owes about $2,000 on the cards at any given time. Where do you fit in?

Trying to determine how many cards you should carry depends upon your individual circumstances. If your finances are in good shape and you are starting to do quite a bit of business traveling and entertaining, you want to make sure you have enough cards to take care of all that business conveniently. If, on the other hand, you often find yourself strapped for cash or charging things more often than you feel comfortable doing, it is time to start cutting back.

At an absolute minimum, you really need only one bank card to survive quite adequately in our society. Having one card with a reasonable credit limit of $1,000 or $2,000 should be more than enough to carry you through basic transactions. These include making hotel reservations, renting cars, getting tickets for various events over the telephone, making purchases for which you don't have cash handy, and having that little bit of extra cash in case of an emergency. Many people go through their entire lives with just one card without feeling in the least bit inconvenienced.

If you have only one card, a bank card (Visa or MasterCard) is your best bet. These cards are still accepted more widely than other cards, and if you are careful about your payments and annual fees, you can get a card that costs you relatively little.

If you also want the convenience of not worrying about having enough cash every time you get gas, keep a gasoline credit card as well. As stated in chapter 1, these are not to difficult to get, and if you watch yourself, keeping gas charges in line should not be too much of a problem. Whether you are starting out fresh, recovering from financial ruin, or just don't want to tempt yourself with too many cards, having these two cards should cover you well in most situations.

If you do a lot of travel either for business or personal reasons, or if restaurant dining and higher profile cultural events are a large part of your life, you might want to consider a travel and entertainment card. While

Diners Club and Carte Blanche are certainly still viable, American Express is the leader here. You have to be willing to pay a high annual fee (American Express is currently running at $55), and you won't be able to carry your charges over to the following month, but as a help for record keeping and doing away with the need to carry around a lot of cash for various social situations, a travel and entertainment card can't be beat.

Always keep in mind the small but insidious factor that comes into play when you have more than one or two cards: keeping track of your monthly debt is that much harder. Not because you can't do the math but because, as a distraught cardowner says, "After a while, I was afraid to add it all up. If I kept all the charges separate, they didn't seem so bad, and I could convince myself that things were still manageable."

Beyond these basics, the choice is up to you. You can add department store cards to further increase shopping convenience, but remember, if you are prone to cheering yourself up with shopping sprees, nothing is more deadly than a credit card at your favorite department store. The worse you feel, the more you charge. As far as getting more bank or travel and entertainment cards is concerned, whether regular or gold, do so if finances are not a problem, you want a higher credit limit overall, or one of the many marketing gimmicks now being offered seems like something you could use.

6

Traveling Abroad with Credit Cards

Credit cards can be a great aid to traveling abroad. While you will obviously still need cash for those street vendors, out-of-the-way bistros, and some foreign conveniences, your standard credit card can be used to pay for most major items. This includes hotels and airplane tickets as well as many of the more established stores and restaurants.

Yet this ability to charge big as well as inconsequential items can create problems of its own. Before you pack your favorite charge card and then blithely start charging away, remember that banks can withhold a certain portion of your credit limit if big-ticket items suddenly start appearing on your account. Banks do this to protect themselves, withholding that portion until the expensive charges have been paid off.

If this happens while you are traveling, you may have a major problem on your hands. The last thing you want is to find out that you've reached your "limit" in the middle of the trip, when according to your careful calculations, you still have plenty of charging power left. To protect yourself, before you leave check your credit limit on the card you plan to take; call the bank that issued the card and find out whether such a policy would be applicable to you. If your relationship to your bank is good, see if you can get your credit limit raised to accommodate your trip. If that doesn't work, some experts advise to bring two cards: one for those big-ticket items and one for day-to-day spending purposes.

As you make decisions about how much cash or traveler's checks you want to take versus how much you intend to pay by card, remember that both have their costs. American Express, for example, charges a one percent commission on all traveler's checks you purchase. If you think you'll save yourself some money by paying with a credit card, think again; many charge companies tack on a one percent commission for converting foreign currency into dollars. To further complicate matters, remember that all currencies fluctuate; when you leave the one percent commission up to your credit card company, you also have no control over the conversion rate on which this commission is based.

Some other things to consider regarding credit cards when you are going on a trip:

- **Service**. American Express is still the undisputed leader in this area, with its name recognition and world wide offices providing all types of services, including replacing lost cards quickly. Some of the services that American Express provides are:
- A network of offices in more than 1,700 locations in 120 countries; services include: making reservations, cashing traveler's checks, accepting payments on monthly statements, receiving mail, replacing lost cards
- An 800-number hotline for emergencies and for relaying messages
- American Express traveler's checks can be ordered by phone

As the credit card wars heat up, MasterCard and Visa gold cards are providing many of the same services, including their own 800-number hotline. If you are a frequent traveler, this upgrade in services is a legitimate reason to consider a gold card.

- **Credit limit.** Credit limit problems are not limited to cards with revolving credit. While one of the selling points of American Express is that it has no credit limit, as mentioned, it is monitored. To forestall any problems, make a call ahead of time to make sure there will be no limits placed on your card.

- **Acceptance.** Visa and MasterCard are accepted in more places than American Express, which tends to be favored by the more prestige-conscious vendors. Depending on your charge patterns, this may be another reason to consider taking two cards.

• **Rebates.** The credit card wars are producing various travel-related bonuses, such as the Membership Miles program. If you do a lot of traveling, that can add up. MasterCard and Visa are introducing their own bonuses. If you have a number of cards, be sure to check on such rebates; they can make charging your trip not only convenient, but that much better for your own finances.

PART III

Debt

7

Keeping Solvent and Fixing Your Credit Report

Jim and Joanne decided to purchase a garden center that had just come on the market. They enjoyed landscaping their own property, and since the previous owner of the center had already built up a steady clientele, the chance to open up their own business seemed a chance worth taking. Needing some money for the purchase, they got a home equity loan. The interest rates were low, they had a little money saved to start with, and with their combined talents they were sure they could make a go of it. Unfortunately, the economy in their part of the country took a downturn, and the disposable income people had for plants and shrubbery suddenly went for necessities. Jim and Joanne spent their savings and, fearing the loss of their home, suddenly found themselves borrowing more money just to keep up with their home equity payments.

When Maryann got her first MasterCard, she was very good about keeping up with monthly payments and never owed a cent of interest. Although her salary at the library where she worked was not great, she managed to buy only what she could afford. However, going through a difficult time, Maryann decided to buy a VCR on credit. She couldn't afford the $400 price tag but justified the purchase by saying she deserved to do something nice for herself and vowing to pay back the charge promptly. However, suddenly enjoying the opportunities of purchasing on credit, she didn't. Instead, she bought a few other things with her card, took out some sizable cash advances during some vacations, and, when she lost her job, needed to borrow more money just to keep up. Before she knew it she was eight thousand dollars in debt.

These people did not act recklessly—at least not in the beginning. Jim and Joanne's purchase of the garden center seemed like the opportunity to fulfill a lifelong dream. Maryann's use of a small credit card purchase to cheer herself up seemed, as she put it, "so innocent at the time." Yet in both cases, unforeseen events and miscalculations escalated into big problems. What happened to all of them represents the kinds of financial traps that millions of adults, young and old, have fallen into in the last few years. Such traps carry heavy financial and emotional burdens. Jim and Joanne ended up nearly losing their home, while it took Maryann years before she felt solvent again.

These stories, and many like them, show how crucial it is to manage debt carefully. Things can quickly go awry even with the best intentions. And while letting debt pile up and run away from you seems to happen easily, the opposite—whittling the debt down to manageable size—is much harder to accomplish.

Signs of Trouble

- You are making debt payments irregularly or are frequently late
- The payments you are making are coming from secondary or windfall sources (a second job, a certificate of deposit that comes due, interest income)
- You find yourself juggling—choosing whether to pay one bill over another, or choosing whether to pay household bills like rent or food versus credit card payments
- Your debt repayments are above the 20 percent cutoff of your monthly take-home pay
- You are starting to use your credit cards for small, daily purchases such as buying toiletries, small household items, or even going to the movies
- You are making only minimum payments on your credit cards
- You borrow from one card to pay off another
- You buy something on a card (no matter how small the amount) with no idea how you'll pay it back

While together the above items paint a bleak picture, what is so insidious about debt is that usually the problems start in a small way, like Maryann's innocent VCR purchase. Jim and Joanne's home equity loan seemed like a safe bet in the beginning also, until they had to borrow more money "to keep things going for the time being."

The period of slowly increasing debt is very deceptive. Since the problems at the beginning usually don't seem overwhelming, one can justify new loans and new credit card charges with the expectation of future improvement. In addition, mail solicitations for quick cash and new cards come along because your credit rating is usually still good. All of these offers of new credit are hard to turn down—until everything snowballs and you are borrowing money just to stay afloat.

Maryann explained the dilemma perfectly: "When things got tough, I used my credit cards to prop myself up—a little bit here and a little there to get me through the lean times. It seemed perfectly legitimate, and I could go forever borrowing from one card to pay another without spending a dime of my own money. It's all very self-deceiving."

Pay attention to those bad habits. Taken in isolation they may not seem like much, but they add up very quickly and cause you to be overwhelmed and plunge even further into debt.

Getting Back on Track

To get on top of your debt, *planning* is key. In paying back any kind of loan, you have to decide in advance how much of the loan you will pay back and on what kind of schedule you will do this. When you get an installment loan from a bank, this is easier to do because you will decide on monthly repayments with your loan officer before you get a penny of the money. Just remember, however, that the agreement you sign is a binding document. If you don't make your payments (sometimes skipping just one is enough), anything you may have pledged as collateral can legally be taken away, and your credit rating is ruined as well.

Having a plan means thinking through carefully what you can afford to pay every month and sticking to it. Many people, suddenly hit by the horrible realization that they are in debt, immediately try to pay back large amounts of any outstanding balances. This all-or-nothing approach is counterproductive; more often than not they have paid back more than they can really afford and within months they are borrowing more money to get caught up again.

Never borrow more money to repay debts—it's a prescription for disaster. Instead, first think of other alternatives: Is there any other way to come up with the income? A second job? Cutting back on expenses? While difficult, cutting back in lifestyle is often a viable alternative for many people in debt. This can include eating meals in instead of out, spending less on entertainment, not buying as many new clothes as you would like.

With credit card debt, you have some additional concerns. Many people wonder whether they should cut up all their credit cards. Unless you find yourself totally out of control, you would be wise to take intermittent steps first. Cut up all credit cards except the one with the lowest interest rate; use it for those occasions when a credit card really does come in handy. To avoid temptation, take the card out of your wallet and keep it in a special place either at home or outside the home, such as in a bank safety deposit box where you may keep other valuables. That way, your card will be available for emergencies or other needed purchases—what you will cut down on is charging purchases on the spur of the moment, which is so deadly to many people.

Remember, when you are getting rid of your cards for any reason, it's not enough just to cut them up and forget about them. You have to inform the card issuer that you are closing the account. Do it in writing to best protect yourself and have a record of it. This way, the issuer will inform the credit card bureau that your account is officially closed, and you won't have to worry about any unresolved items on your credit report that may cause problems in the future.

Even if you do not cut up your cards, you will probably be needing to change some well-ingrained habits. Think twice before you buy anything on credit—pay by check or cash instead. It may take a little extra time and effort—you won't be able to buy things over the phone, you will have to carry cash around or make sure there is enough money in your checking account—but it will be more than worth it.

Doing it the other way around, that is, paying by credit card and then promising to pay back the same amount when the bill comes, just doesn't work. Human nature being what it is, by the time the monthly statement comes, the money apportioned to pay back the charges has long been spent. To convince yourself of this, just think back to the last time you went out to dinner with friends and picked up the tab by paying with your credit card. You collected money from everyone, yet how much of it went into the bank or as a repayment for any bills? Chances are, your answer is zero.

Another trick to help yourself manage credit card payments is to deduct what you charged from your checking or savings account, as if you really had spent the money. Seeing it in black and white will reinforce the fact that you will owe that amount on your next statement; it will also make it harder to be lulled into a false sense of security by spending money you don't really have.

The National Foundation for Consumer Credit

If you find yourself in over your head and don't know how to begin to solve your credit problems, you have places to turn to for help. The National Foundation for Consumer Credit located in Silver Spring, Maryland, and Consumer Credit Counseling Services (CCCS), which are local organizations affiliated with the National Foundation, will help you out.

Consumer Credit Counseling Services are nonprofit organizations supported by banks, merchants, and other businesses to provide a helpful way for consumers to work out their finances. There are counseling services in over 600 communities in the country, and they charge either no fee or a very small fee for helping out. You set up an appointment with a budget counselor and go over your financial status. If warranted, the counselor may advise you to consolidate all your loans into one loan at a lower interest rate and use that money to pay back all your charges. Your counselor also gives you budgeting tips, helping you to prevent problems in the future. This work may require one appointment or several.

To find out about counseling services near you, call the National Foundation's toll-free number (1-800-388-2227). They will send a pamphlet giving you more information about their services and the steps you can take to get yourself back into financial health.

Credit Repair Clinics

Beware of credit repair clinics! Supposedly created to help people deal with improving their credit ratings and resolving other intimidating financial matters, credit repair clinics often promise what they cannot deliver. And they do so at hefty fees of hundreds of dollars. As opposed to the Consumer Credit Counseling Services, they are definitely for-profit businesses.

Credit repair clinics argue that they perform a valuable service—helping people deal with credit bureaus, deciphering often complex credit reports, and knowing how to challenge the information in those reports. The fact is, there is really nothing they do that you can't do. Because the law requires that you as a consumer contact a credit bureau directly—you can't do it through a third party—credit repair clinics don't save you as much time and effort as you might think.

As you will see in the section that follows, much is

changing in the industry of credit reporting. The changes will make it easier for the average consumer to learn about his or her credit rating and deal with credit bureaus. If you still feel that you need to go through a credit repair clinic, at least follow this one piece of advice: when checking the prices of the various clinics you find listed in the telephone book, ask them if you can pay for their services *after* they have delivered what they have promised. If they agree, maybe they really can help you.

Dealing with the Credit Reporting Industry —Help for the Consumer

If you've been overwhelmed by debt, missed payments, had a dispute about a payment, or had any other kind of financial trouble, chances are your credit rating has been hurt as well. The remainder of this chapter will show you what to do in such situations. As in other areas of credit, your first defense is to know that you are protected by law. In 1970, Congress passed the Fair Credit Reporting Act to help consumers obtain fair and accurate treatment by the various consumer reporting agencies that gather information on them and sell it to their creditors.

Historically, the Big Three information service companies (TRW, Trans Union, and Equifax) have regarded the credit-granting organizations as their main customers. The consumer, meanwhile, was left out in the cold, and the Federal Trade Commission, the agency that oversees the credit reporting industry, was receiving more and more complaints on credit reporting from consumers. The whole process of getting your credit report was unclear and complicated: getting in touch with those who issued the reports was difficult; you had to pay money to get your report unless you had just been denied credit; the report was complex and full of various symbols and codes. There were also many mixups—such as Joe Smith Jr. from Maine being mistaken for Joe Smith Sr. in Arkansas—and resolving the information on mixed-up credit reports sometimes seemed impossible.

The credit bureaus claimed that the problems were caused by various factors. In the first place, the volume of reports generated was daunting: 1.5 million credit reports a day translates into 450 million reports per year. Naturally there would be some problems. Another big factor was the fast pace of the electronic revolution. In trying to update computer software as well as ironing out existing kinks, new problems were created and mixups occurred.

In 1991, a number of states along with the Federal Trade Commission sued TRW. The lawsuit was settled that same year with TRW agreeing to various changes that would help the consumer get quicker and more accurate credit reports. The other two companies made changes as well. In addition, Congress began taking another look at the Fair Credit Reporting Act to see how it could be updated to keep pace with technological changes and strengthen consumer rights.

All these developments are good for the consumer. It means that the credit bureaus are now beginning to think of the consumer as their customer, along with the companies to which they give your credit history. So many changes will take a few years to sort themselves out, but progress is already being made, with bureaus instituting 800 numbers, for example, and lowering their prices for obtaining credit reports. TRW has announced that you will be able to obtain one free credit report per year. Upon request, the credit reporting agencies will also send you pamphlets explaining how the credit information they have on you is used and how to read your credit report. You will find detailed information on how to contact the credit reporting agencies, as well as their current prices and procedures, in the appendix of resources.

If you desire more information on the credit reporting industry write to the Federal Trade Commission under whose purview the credit reporting industry falls. Another excellent source of information is Associated Credit Bureaus, Inc., an international trade association that represents more than 1,000 credit reporting agencies. Established in 1906, it has an ongoing public relations program to help educate the consumer on credit and credit reporting. It will send you free pamphlets on such issues as your right to privacy in relation to credit reports, ethical concerns in credit reporting, and information about the credit industry in general; it also provides a helpful list of words and definitions often used in credit reporting.

How to Get Your Credit Report

Always remember that you have a right to see what is in your credit report. Knowing that your credit report is not "somewhere out there," but a document you can inspect and make changes to if necessary, gives you a measure of control over something that affects many areas of your life. And those areas are extensive. Besides you and the credit reporting company, others who have access to your records include:

- Anyone who is considering extending credit to you
- A potential employer
- A potential insurer
- Anyone with a "legitimate business need"

As you can see, negative or incorrect information on your credit report can affect much more than getting a loan. As the information in the computers of the credit reporting companies gathers over the years, the margin for error grows as well. Keep in mind that not all credit bureaus have your records—it depends on which services are subscribed to by those who grant you credit. Nevertheless, make it a point to periodically inspect your credit rating; this may take some calling around before you find out who has what information on you, but it may save you from potentially embarrassing or frustrating situations in the future.

If you are denied credit by anyone, you have a right to see your credit report, free. Also, whoever denies you credit has to tell you whether a credit report was used in evaluating your situation, as well as the name and address of any credit reporting agency supplying the report. You must request the report within 30 days of receiving your denial notice to get it without paying a fee. Do everything in writing, both for your own record keeping and to best secure any legal protection to which you are entitled.

You have a right to find out the sources of the information on your credit reports. In addition, the credit reporting agency has to tell you who has been sent a credit report in the last six months; if potential employers have received this information, you have a right to know who they were within the last two years.

Fixing Your Credit Report

Consider the following scenario:

Like Jim and Joanne, the unfortunate landscape architects, you are starting your own business. You buy yourself a computer (with a credit card) to help with your work. Within a week the computer starts malfunctioning. The manufacturer promises to replace it within days, which it does, but the second computer has similar problems. Angry, you stop payment on the credit card bill for the amount of the computer, telling your bank that you won't pay until all the problems with your computer have been taken care of.

The following month's statement includes the disputed amount, along with added interest charges. As you fight with your bank trying to get the disputed amount wiped off your monthly statement, you are also trying to work out a solution with the computer manufacturer. This goes on for a couple of months. Finally, you get the computer you want. You pay the disputed amount of your credit card bill and, after a few months, even get the extra interest charges deducted from your account.

You forget the whole incident. About a year later, needing money to stimulate your business, you apply for a loan. To your surprise, you are denied it, though until that point, as far as you knew, your credit history was good. You try to get other loans, but they are denied also. Only later, when you began sorting out matters, do you get a copy of your credit report and see that you have been listed as delinquent for not paying for the computer or the interest charges that had accrued. If you had known about this, you could have had your credit report corrected and the "delinquency" explained. How?

If you notice what appears to be incorrect information in your credit report, you can tell the credit reporting company to conduct an investigation. *Note:* It is up to the credit reporting company to verify that the information in its report is correct. If it cannot do that, the information must be deleted. This is another important right you have: the burden of proof is on the credit reporting agency, not you. (The consumer reporting company doesn't have to do an investigation if it has "reasonable" cause to believe that your request is "frivolous" or "irrelevant.")

Suppose, however, the credit reporting agency comes back to you and says that upon completing the investigation, it has found all the information to be correct. If you still disagree, you have a right to compose a 100-word summary of your version of events and to have that summary added to the credit report. In addition, you have a right to request that a new credit report, either as corrected by the reporting company or with your 100-word summary, be sent out to anyone who received the report in the past six months (or the last two years if the report was sent regarding employment).

Whether disputed or not, negative information cannot stay on a credit report for longer than seven years. The one major exception is bankruptcy, which can be reported for ten years.

8

The Bottom Line: Facing Debt Collectors and Declaring Bankruptcy

Not being able to make debt payments is a difficult situation to be in. Not only are you trying to deal with an unpleasant financial situation, but you are grappling with the emotional burden as well.

"I was ashamed that I had gotten myself into this mess," explains Corrine, a New York stage actress who found herself borrowing more and more on her credit cards to make ends meet. "Feeling ashamed is deadly. I had come to the Big Apple to make it big, and instead the only thing I accomplished was piling up my credit card debt. I felt so bad about it, I couldn't face the problem, and consequently I borrowed more money to cover up the debts I had."

Corrine puts her finger on the underlying reason why so many people can't get off the debt merry-go-round: the shame accompanying the problem. Studies indicate that the majority of people who find themselves on the receiving end of a debt collector's call do so not because they borrowed money with no intention ever to pay it back, but because of poor financial planning mixed with unforeseen circumstances such as job loss or medical emergencies. They want to think of themselves as responsible, competent adults. When the financial problems come, they have a hard time separating the problem from their sense of self-worth.

"I remember once I got a call from a collector who sounded like the stereotypical Marine sergeant," Corinne recounts. "He knew exactly how to make me feel humiliated, and I still cringe when I remember it."

The shame game, as Corinne refers to it, is a game "in which you are the loser. The first step in coming to terms with my debt was realizing I didn't have to play it anymore."

Taking this step is not easy by any means, whether you are making your first call to a collection agency, to a lawyer, or to your creditor to try to reschedule debt payments. But it is crucial in getting yourself back to financial health. Know that *you are not your debt.* You have made one—or many—mistakes, but no matter how bad the situation, there are ways to solve any problem, no matter how dire. Just as in other areas of credit, laws and regulations have been passed that address this very issue. While acknowledging your responsibility for getting into debt and repaying it to the best of your abilities, these laws also give you certain rights and protections and recognize the fact that you don't have to play the shame game forever.

Contacting Your Creditor

If you have just started receiving letters from the bank or finance company saying you are behind in your payments, you have an excellent chance of resolving matters. The first step is to contact the bank before it turns over your account to a collection agency. This contact is very important, because it shows your creditor that you are making a real effort to take care of the situation. Someone who contacts a creditor directly is saying, "I've been having problems, but I want to pay back what I'm able. Can we discuss it?"

Many people refuse to take this step, hiding behind the excuse that nowadays everything is taken care of by computer anyway. They feel there's no use talking to the creditor because they imagine the creditor as an emotionless piece of electronic equipment demanding payment of such and such amount by such and such a date—with no leeway for anyone who can't keep on schedule. It's not true. As much as our work and record keeping is now done by machines, as much as big corporations have taken over many industries, it is useful to remember that behind those machines in the corporations are people making decisions. If anything, your call to a creditor is an attempt to get beyond the machines to the people in charge.

Also remember that creditors don't particularly like going to collection agencies—if purely on financial grounds. Collectors typically work on commission, earning an average of a quarter or a third of the amount they collect. If a creditor can do so in a manner that seems reasonable, he would be happier to work out the problem with you. In addition, remember that a creditor wants your business—as long as you keep your account in good standing and are able to pay the bills.

If you get someone who is understanding on the line when you call your creditor, tell them your problem and reiterate that you would like to pay what you can. They may ask you to discuss things further or direct you to a budget counseling service such as CCCS. Listen to what these people have to say. You don't lose anything by trying. If you can work things out to the satisfaction of all parties, you will rest easier and not hurt your credit rating either.

Collection Agencies

If you have ignored your creditor's attempts to contact you, chances are you'll next be hearing from a collection agency. Your major disadvantage in dealing with a collection agency is that, as opposed to your creditor, a collection agency is not as concerned about maintaining your goodwill. Since collection agencies work on commission, they want you to pay up—so when you start getting calls and letters from a collection agency, expect more pressure than you received from your creditor.

Don't allow yourself to be intimidated. The Fair Debt Collection Practices Act was passed in 1977 to protect you in dealing with collection agencies.* Unlike other legislation, the Fair Debt Collection Practices Act is quite specific in spelling out what a collection agency can or cannot do in its dealings with you. Become acquainted with the specifics that follow:

- **Initial contact.** To locate you, a collection agency is permitted to contact anyone who it believes can reasonably help find you. However, this contact has to be discreet; that is, the agency cannot discuss the debt or its particulars with these people. It is legally permissible to contact such people only once, except if the agency believes it has been given "erroneous" or "incomplete" information.

When a collection agency contacts you, there are certain pieces of information it must give you, either when you first hear from them or within five days. This information must be in writing and contain:

- Amount of the debt
- Name of the creditor to whom the debt is owed
- Statement that says you have thirty days to dispute the validity of the debt or any portion of it
- Statement that says if you do dispute the debt within thirty days, in writing, the collection

---

*Interestingly enough, the Fair Debt Collection Practices Act protects you against collection agencies—nothing is said about creditors themselves. However, in the rare instance that a creditor starts doing what has been outlawed for collection agencies, contact a lawyer. The creditor won't get away with it either.

agency will have to get verification of it before continuing its collection efforts

The collection agency must also give you the name and address of the original creditor, if by any chance it differs from the current creditor. The law puts the burden on the collection agency to have its facts straight so that you will not be unnecessarily bothered.

You should also know that you have the right to request that a collection agency stop contacting you. If you do this—in writing—the agency can only contact you to tell you that some further action is being taken, it cannot continue its efforts to try to make you pay.

• **Communicating with the debtor.** The law also provides strict guidelines the collection agency must follow in its communications with you. It is not allowed to contact you at any "unusual" or "inconvenient" place. The hours of contact are strictly enforced as well: you can only be contacted between 8 A.M. and 9 P.M. If you work an evening or night shift and give the collection agency alternate times that would be more convenient, the agency must adhere to them.

The collection agency is also forbidden to contact you at work if you write a letter saying that your employer prohibits you from receiving such a communication. In order to protect yourself from the possibility of an agency contacting your employer before you expressly forbid it, write the letter as soon as you get your first contact from the agency.

The guidelines also expressly forbid any kind of harassment or abuse. Examples of harassment that is not allowed are:

- Use or threat of violence
- Threatening your property
- Use of obscene or profane language
- Threatening your reputation or publicizing your name as a debtor (in a newspaper ad, for example)
- Advertising to sell your debt as a way to coerce you to pay
- Causing the telephone to ring repeatedly or calling and then hanging up without revealing who is on the line
- Making you pay for collect calls or telegrams

Other guidelines fall under the general heading of false or misleading representations. Examples of deceptive practices forbidden to the collection agency are:

- The implication that the collection agency is affiliated with the government in any way, either federal or state
- Misstating the amount or circumstances of any debt
- Using a false name or lying about the services the collection agency provides
- Falsely implying that you have committed a crime and that nonpayment of the debt will result in your arrest, imprisonment, or seizure of property when no such action has been legally taken
- Using government or court stationery to intimidate you

If you have been contacted by a collection agency at this point, you may consider hiring an attorney. The law expressly states that if you tell the collection agency to contact your attorney and provide the attorney's name and address, the collection agency is prohibited from contacting you further. If you feel a collection agency has acted illegally, you can sue and collect up to $1,000 in damages, as well as payment for court costs and attorney fees. In the case of a class action suit, up to $500,000 in damages can be awarded.

The collection agency is also prohibited from contacting third parties, such as friends, relatives, or neighbors in order to publicize your debt and put more pressure on you to repay it.

• **Where to go with complaints.** If you feel that a collection agent has been acting improperly, write a letter to the manager or president of the agency, stating that you know your rights and outlining the abuse or harassment you have received. As with all such mail, send it certified.

If you feel you need to take further recourse, other places to contact include:

- Your local Better Business Bureau or consumer protection agency
- Your state attorney general's office (states also have various guidelines on debt collection)

You can also send a letter to the Division of Credit Practices at the Federal Trade Commission. The commission will not represent you in any dispute, but it will provide more information and steer you to helpful resources.

Bankruptcy—When to Consider It

Bankruptcy is protection—legal, financial, emotional. Yet it should never be undertaken lightly. While it provides a clean start for someone who has too many debts to pay, the consequences of declaring bankruptcy affect you for years, destroying your chances of getting credit and even influencing such things as employment or getting an apartment.

If you find yourself so far over your head in debt, the drastic step of declaring bankruptcy may be your only solution. It protects you from being sued by your creditors and, depending on the circumstances, safeguards your assets. You may not be able to get more credit, but at least you can stop dodging the bill collectors and get off that treadmill of spending more and more money to pay back loans and never feeling caught up. For many, the lifting of that emotional burden is more than worth any of the negative consequences bankruptcy entails. As Corinne, the actress, said when she finally threw in the towel and declared bankruptcy: "I couldn't stand it any longer. Trying to chip away at that mountain of debt, having no idea of the things I was paying for anymore, became excruciating. I almost had a nervous breakdown."

Corinne wouldn't have been alone. Agonizing about the moral and financial issues of paying back huge debts, many people suffer nervous breakdowns or even commit suicide because they have no idea how they will cope. Bankruptcy provides a way out—before one gets to that extreme.

Some people are afraid to explore bankruptcy because they still associate it with shame. But as discussed at the beginning of this chapter, feeling ashamed only causes more problems. The bankruptcy code exists for a reason: it outlines ways to resolve your financial problems when they reach the point of unmanageability.

Think of it this way: in declaring bankruptcy, you are not running away. Rather, you are accepting both the negative consequences and benefits that will come from such a step. Like the 700,000-plus individuals who declared bankruptcy in 1990, you are taking a responsible step rather than doing something hurtful to yourself and your loved ones.

Don't make the decision to declare bankruptcy alone. Contact a lawyer who specializes in the field; if you can't afford one, there are other counseling organizations, such as the Consumer Credit Counseling Services (see appendix) that will help you make the right decision. If you are considering bankruptcy, here are some questions to ask yourself:

• **Is your income steady?** If it is, chances are greater that you don't have to go the bankruptcy route. With the help of a professional, you may be able to figure a way to consolidate your debts or work out lower payments with your creditors.

• **What is the difference between your debt load and your income?** A professional will help you figure out how long it will take to pay off whatever you owe. In some cases, it may take so long that the emotional and financial toll will just not be worth it. Or your monthly payments will be so low that your credit rating will be ruined anyway.

- **Is your financial picture improving or getting worse?** If things are really getting better, you just might be able to hold on a little while longer and slowly get yourself out of the hole. However, be careful of this prosperity-is-right-around-the-corner attitude. Make sure things really are improving—that you're not just giving into wishful thinking. Otherwise you will postpone taking necessary steps to get yourself back on track.

Chapter 7 vs. Chapter 13

Based on regulations set forth in the Federal Bankruptcy Code, your declaration of bankruptcy can take one of two forms: Chapter 7 or Chapter 13. Chapter 7 is more drastic and entails liquidating your assets and selling them off to pay your creditors. Chapter 13 is a rescheduling of your debts—you pay them off by working out a repayment plan under the auspices of the court. But you get to keep your assets. Both chapters protect you from further action by your creditors or collection agencies.

- **Chapter 7.** About two-thirds of the people who file for bankruptcy do so under Chapter 7. Your debts are wiped out, the court appoints a trustee, and the trustee sells off your assets, using the money to pay back the creditors.

It is important to remember that not all of your assets are repossessed. What you can keep is governed by state law. Generally, you can keep all household appliances, goods, and apparel. In discussing your options with a lawyer, be sure to have clear in your mind exactly what your state law allows.

You should also know that even if you declare bankruptcy, you will have to continue to carry some debts. These include: alimony, child support, student loans, and unpaid taxes.

• **Chapter 13.** If you have a steady source of income, but need to give yourself breathing space to repay all your debts, Chapter 13 may provide the right option. Under Chapter 13 you get three years to repay your debts; in certain circumstances, this time frame can be extended two more years. During this time you are legally protected from your creditors and the bothersome pressure of collection agencies.

Since your assets are not repossessed, you don't have to worry about how much of your possessions you get to keep. However, just as under Chapter 7, there are certain debts that you still have to carry.

Filing for Bankruptcy

Corinne, who ended up declaring bankruptcy, describes it as a long process. The most important step, of course, is deciding to face the problem, admitting that your debts are not manageable. After that comes the research: seeing lawyers for free advice, getting debt counseling, finding out if bankruptcy is your only option. If you decide that it is, proceed by hiring a lawyer, which can range from four or five hundred dollars (for paperwork and court costs) to over a thousand.

Once the decision has been made to go ahead, you start the filing process. Corinne's experience is typical of the steps involved. The steps involved are:

1. The actual filing of the paperwork. This consists of approximately twenty pages of forms—affidavits declaring your current assets, total debt, plus a complete listing of all creditors owed and what amounts are owed to each at the time of the filing.

2. After the papers have been filed, you will get a notice from the court that the papers have been received; you are also informed of the "docket date," which is the date a few months down the road when you will appear in court for your hearing.

3. Another step after filing is calling your creditors and telling them you are filing for bankruptcy. Depending on your arrangement with your lawyer, he or she may do this for you. If any creditors or collection agents call at this point, you can give them your lawyer's number; once you have done this, it is illegal for them to contact you again at home.

4. Your court hearing—you can either appear alone or with your lawyer. During this hearing the judge will ask you a number of questions: What made it impossible for you to repay your debt? What assets do you have currently? Is any money coming your way in the near future? The judge may also ask for clarification on current income or employment.

5. After the hearing, your creditors are given copies

of the bankruptcy filing. This allows them time to respond and dispute anything they may find untrue or misleading.

6. A number of months after that, the court issues your final decree.

It is important to remember that, under both chapters, if the court discovers at any time that you are hiding income or in any way have lied about your ability to repay your creditors, your bankruptcy rights can be revoked. Committing bankruptcy fraud is a felony.

Bankruptcy—The Pluses and Minuses

For Corinne, the difficulties of going through the bankruptcy process have been more than worth it. "The immediate relief was wonderful. Not worrying that the ringing telephone signaled another collection agency asking about payment made it all worthwhile." Besides the immediate relief, the feeling of having an official second chance at getting things going again is a very strong palliative for most people.

In terms of credit, of course, the consequences are considerable. Bankruptcy stays on a credit rating for ten years and makes it virtually impossible to get any kind of credit. In some cases, say when a large loan is being considered, creditors can search back for even a longer period of time. Apart from those who give you loans, the other parties that are privy to credit reports, such as potential employers and insurers, can also have negative reactions to whatever business dealings they may be considering with you.

Appendix

Resources

Bankcard Holders of America
560 Herndon Parkway, Suite 120
Herndon, Virginia 22070
1-703-481-1110
A nonprofit consumer group dedicated to education and advocacy for credit card holders.

For information on the Speakers Bureau, call: 1-703-481-1110.

For budgeting and credit counseling:

National Foundation for Consumer Credit/Consumer Credit Counseling Services
8611 2nd Avenue, Suite 100
Silver Spring, Maryland 20910
1-800-388-CCCS (2227)
Nonprofit organization that will provide free or low-cost budgeting advice on loan re-

payment. Call this toll-free number for pamphlets and more information.

On credit unions:

Credit Union National Association
Public Relations/Marketing
P.O. Box 431
Madison, Wisconsin 53701
The national association for state credit leagues. If you write to them, they will provide lists of credit unions nearest you, information on joining a credit union or organizing your own.

Government agencies:

Federal Deposit Insurance Corporation
Office of Consumer Affairs
550 17th Street, N.W.
Washington, D.C. 20429
1-800-424-5488

The federal government's banking regulatory agency will send pamphlets on various credit laws and how they affect you. Also provides information on other consumer and deposit insurance matters.

Federal Trade Commission
6th & Pennsylvania Avenue, N.W.
Washington, D.C. 20580
1-202-326-2222

The federal agency overseeing the consumer reporting and debt collection industries. Will send you pamphlets on the Fair Credit and Reporting Act and the Fair Debt Collection Practices Act. It has regional offices in Atlanta, Boston, Chicago, Cleveland, Dallas, Denver, Los Angeles, New York, San Francisco, and Seattle.

On mail and telephone rights with credit cards:

Direct Marketing Association
11 West 42nd Street
New York, N.Y. 10036-8096
1-212-768-7277

Among other services, of-fers help and information on using credit cards over the telephone, mail-order purchases, and reducing unsolicited mail.

For reducing unsolicited mail, write to:

Mail Preference Service
c/o Direct Marketing Assoc.
11 West 42nd Street,
P.O. Box 3861
New York, N.Y. 10163-3861

For reducing telephone sales:

Telephone Preference Service
c/o Direct Marketing Assoc.
11 West 42nd Street,
P.O. Box 3861
New York, N.Y. 10163–3861

For help with mail order sales write to:

Mail Order Action Line
c/o Direct Marketing Assoc.
6 East 43rd Street
New York, N.Y. 10017–4646

For credit reporting:

Associated Credit Bureaus, Inc.
1090 Vermont Avenue, Suite

200
Washington, D.C. 20005–4905
1-202-371-0910
The international trade association representing credit reporting agencies, it will send you free information on various topics related to the credit reporting industry.

The Big Three Credit Reporting Agencies:

Equifax Credit Information Services
5505 Peachtree-Dunwoody Road
P.O. Box 740256
Atlanta, Georgia 30374–0256
1-800-685-1111
Cost of obtaining your credit report: $8.00

Trans Union Corporation
444 North Michigan Avenue
Chicago, Illinois 60611
1-312-645-0012
(NOTE: No 800 number. If you call the number above, a recording will give you information on how to obtain your credit report. For the future, check with 800-number information, 1-800-555-1212, to see whether an 800 number has been installed.)
Cost of obtaining your credit report: $25 in person, $15 by mail

TRW, Inc.
Marketing Services Division
P.O. Box 850478
Richardson, Texas 75085–0478
1-800-262-7432
(Main office is in Orange, California.)
Cost of obtaining your credit report: 1 free per year, $7.50 each additional